Animal 911
ENVIRONMENTAL THREATS

Animals and Climate Change

NICOLE SHEA

Gareth Stevens
Publishing

Please visit our website, www.garethstevens.com
For a free color catalog of all our high-quality books,
call toll free 1-800-542-2595 or fax 1-877-542-2596.

Library of Congress Cataloging-in-Publication Data

Shea, Nicole.
Animals and climate change / by Nicole Shea.
  p. cm. — (Animal 911: environmental threats)
Includes index.
ISBN 978-1-4339-9703-7 (pbk.)
ISBN 978-1-4339-9704-4 (6-pack)
ISBN 978-1-4339-9702-0 (library binding)
1. Global warming—Juvenile literature. 2. Climatic changes—Juvenile literature. I. Shea, Nicole, 1976- II. Title.
QC981.8.G56 S47 2014
363.7387—dc23

First Edition

Published in 2014 by
Gareth Stevens Publishing
111 East 14th Street, Suite 349
New York, NY 10003

© 2014 Gareth Stevens Publishing

Produced by Planman Technologies
Designed by Sandy Kent
Edited by Jon Bogart

Photo credits: Cover : Susan Miller/ U.S. Fish and Wildlife Service; Background : LeksusTuss/Shutterstock.com; Inside:
Pg 4: Oleg Kiknadze/Shutterstock.com; Pg 5: Jan Martin Will/Shutterstock.com; Pg 7: Yvonne Pijnenburg-Schonewille/
Shutterstock.com; Pg 9: Palo_ok/Shutterstock.com; Pg 10: NASA; Pg 11: Luiz Rocha/Shutterstock.com; Pg 12: ©Andy
Ennis/Alamy/IndiaPicture; Pg 13: Taina Sohlman/Shutterstock.com; Pg 14: Vlad61/Shuterstock.com; Pg 16: Photoshot/
IndiaPicture; Pg 17: Meryll/Shutterstock.com; Pg 18: Ciurzynski/Shutterstock.com; Pg 19: Tom Grundy/Shutterstock.
com; Pg 20: Dmitry Saparov/Shutterstock.com; Pg 21: Debbie Larson/NWS/International Activities/NOAA; Pg 22: Image
by the NASA Scientific Visualization Studio based on data from the Special Sensor Microwave Imager/Sounder (SSMIS)
of the Defense Meteorological Satellite Program (DMSP). Caption based on a story by Maria-José Viñas, NASA Earth
Science News Team; Pg 23: ©ZUMA Wire Service/Alamy/IndiaPicture; Pg 24: Delmas Lehman/Shutterstock.com; Pg 25:
©Stock Connection Blue/Alamy/IndiaPicture; Pg 26: Nialat/Shutterstock; Pg 27: Filip Fuxa/Shutterstock.com; Pg 28: BMJ/
Shutterstock.com; Pg 29: Jacqueline Abromeit/Shutterstock.com; Pg 30: Christian Wilkinson/Shutterstock.com; Pg 31:
Gentoo Multimedia Limited/Shutterstock.com; Pg 32: Photodynamic/Shutterstock.com; Pg 33: ©imagebroker/Alamy/
IndiaPicture; Pg 34: Andaman/Shutterstock.com; Pg 35: ©A & J Visage/Alamy/IndiaPicture; Pg 36: Willyam Bradberry/
Shutterstock.com; Pg 37: Eye Ubiquitous/IndiaPicture; Pg 38: Photoshot/IndiaPicture; Pg 39: ©Anthony Pierce/Alamy/
IndiaPicture; Pg 40: Artem Loskutnikov/Shutterstock.com; Pg 41: Karinkamon/Shutterstock.com; Pg 42: Greendreamz/
Shutterstock.com; Pg 43: Ivan_Sabo/Shutterstock.com; Pg 44: Yuris/Shutterstock.com; Pg 45: ©Jeff Greenberg/Alamy/
IndiaPicture.

Artwork created by Planman Technologies : 6; 8; 15.

Printed in the United States of America

CPSIA compliance information: Batch #CS13GS. For further information contact Gareth Stevens, New York, New York at
1-800-542-2595.

Contents

Words in the glossary appear in **bold** type the first time they are used in the text.

Animals and Climate Change

The polar bear cub watches his mother pace along the edge of the cold water. She is looking for an ice sheet that she and her cub can swim to. They will rest on the ice sheet and use it as a platform to hunt for seals.

The mother polar bear is worried. At first, she does not see any ice sheets. When she does spot one and swims to it, it is too thin to hold her and her cub. She can swim farther out into the cold water to find ice and food, but her cub cannot swim that far.

A mother polar bear hunts for food with her cub.

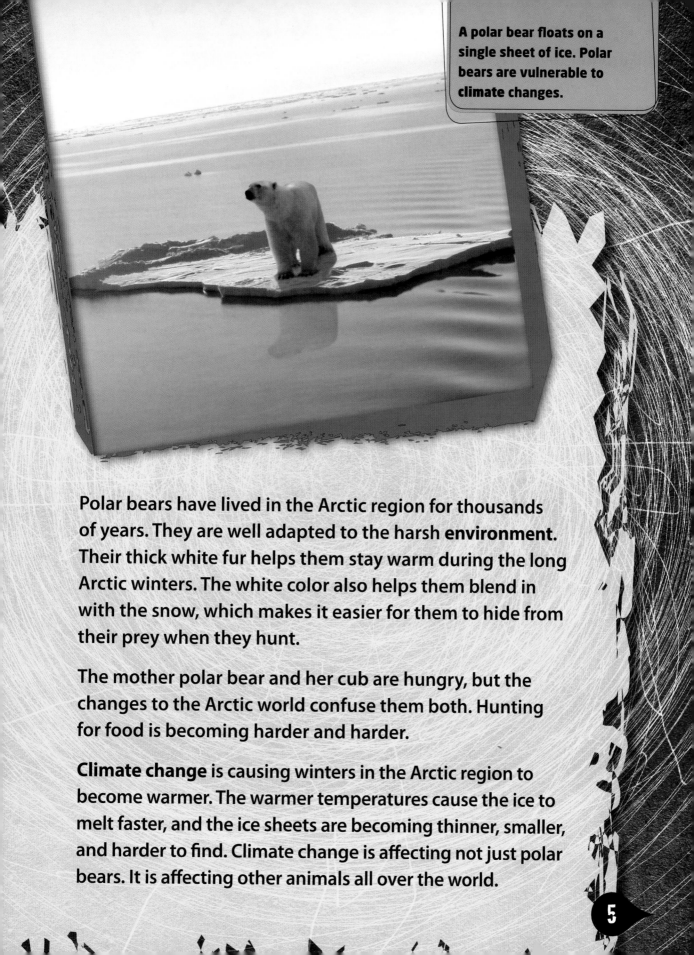

A polar bear floats on a single sheet of ice. Polar bears are vulnerable to climate changes.

Polar bears have lived in the Arctic region for thousands of years. They are well adapted to the harsh **environment**. Their thick white fur helps them stay warm during the long Arctic winters. The white color also helps them blend in with the snow, which makes it easier for them to hide from their prey when they hunt.

The mother polar bear and her cub are hungry, but the changes to the Arctic world confuse them both. Hunting for food is becoming harder and harder.

Climate change is causing winters in the Arctic region to become warmer. The warmer temperatures cause the ice to melt faster, and the ice sheets are becoming thinner, smaller, and harder to find. Climate change is affecting not just polar bears. It is affecting other animals all over the world.

All animals live in a habitat. A habitat is the surroundings in which an animal or a plant naturally lives. Habitats include how an animal hunts for food, builds its home, and raises its young. In fact, how an animal lives depends a lot on the habitat it lives in.

Even small changes in an animal's habitat can result in big changes to the way an animal lives.

This illustration shows how animals share and thrive in the same habitat.

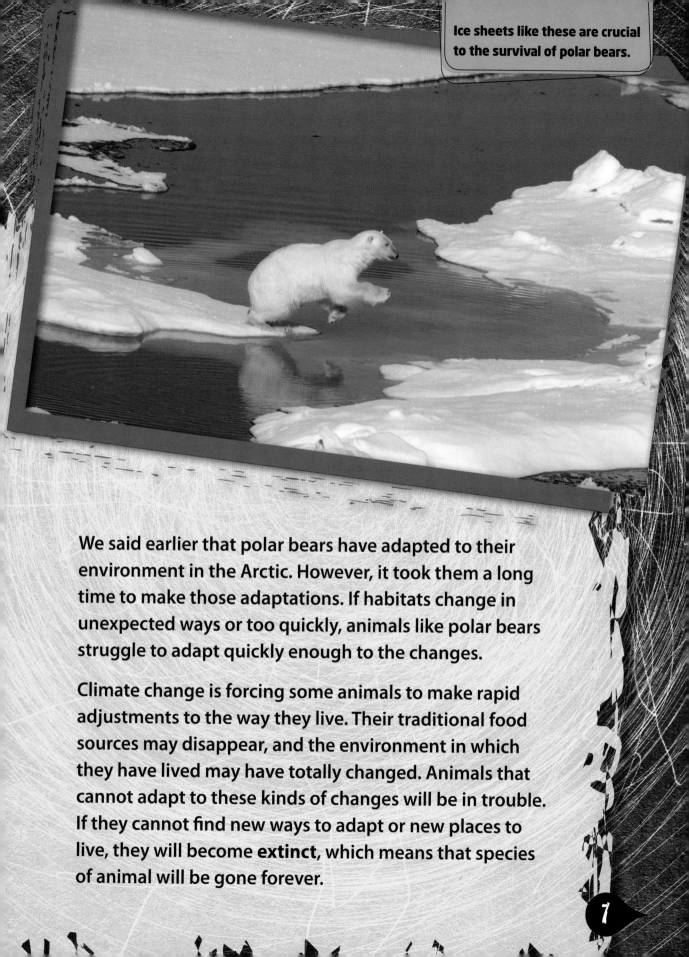

Ice sheets like these are crucial to the survival of polar bears.

We said earlier that polar bears have adapted to their environment in the Arctic. However, it took them a long time to make those adaptations. If habitats change in unexpected ways or too quickly, animals like polar bears struggle to adapt quickly enough to the changes.

Climate change is forcing some animals to make rapid adjustments to the way they live. Their traditional food sources may disappear, and the environment in which they have lived may have totally changed. Animals that cannot adapt to these kinds of changes will be in trouble. If they cannot find new ways to adapt or new places to live, they will become **extinct**, which means that species of animal will be gone forever.

What Is Climate Change?

Weather changes from one day to the next. If it is raining, you take an umbrella to school. If it is cold, you put on a sweater.

Climate is the average weather conditions, measured over a long period of time. Different places on Earth have different climates. Temperature and precipitation (such as rain or snow) are two of the most common ways that scientists compare climates.

Some places are wet and some are dry. Some places are cold and some are hot. Even places that are cold in the winter and hot in the summer can have one kind of climate.

This map of Africa shows its climate zones.

Climate Zones

- Mediterranean Zone
- Semi-arid Zone
- Tropical Zone with Dry Seasons
- Humid Tropical Zone
- Equatorial Zone
- Desert Zone

Because of climate change, some areas of the planet have become hotter and drier.

Just as climate is weather measured over a long period of time, climate change is also measured over a long period of time. One cool summer or even a few warm winters is not enough to determine if climate change is happening. Scientists review data that includes information for longer than 50 years.

One change scientists have seen is a rise in temperature of the whole Earth, about 1.4°F (.77°C) in the 1900s. This increase is very small but, as we will see, even small changes in temperature can have a big effect on weather and the animals that depend on it.

What Causes Climate Change?

Throughout its history, Earth's climate has changed very much. The planet was very warm when dinosaurs lived here. During the Ice Age, Earth was much cooler. Animals such as the woolly mammoth thrived in the ice and snow.

Some changes happen very slowly, over millions of years. Some changes can be very sudden. A volcano or other major event can cause changes. Through study and research, scientists have discovered much about the world's climate in the past.

Volcano eruptions like this one can affect weather conditions thousands of miles from the volcano.

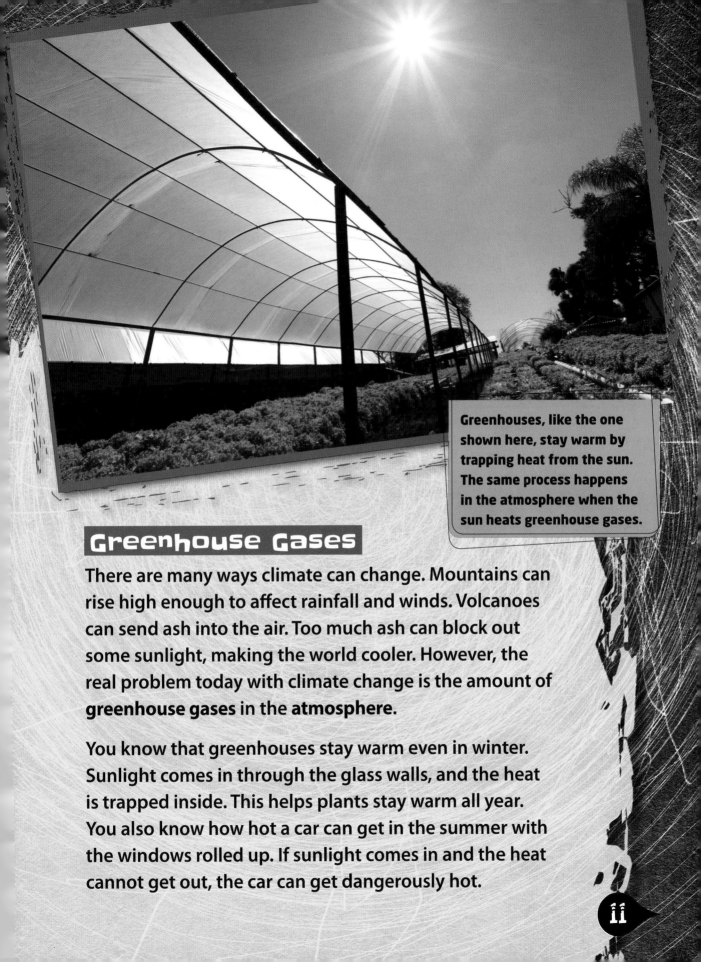

Greenhouses, like the one shown here, stay warm by trapping heat from the sun. The same process happens in the atmosphere when the sun heats greenhouse gases.

Greenhouse Gases

There are many ways climate can change. Mountains can rise high enough to affect rainfall and winds. Volcanoes can send ash into the air. Too much ash can block out some sunlight, making the world cooler. However, the real problem today with climate change is the amount of **greenhouse gases** in the **atmosphere**.

You know that greenhouses stay warm even in winter. Sunlight comes in through the glass walls, and the heat is trapped inside. This helps plants stay warm all year. You also know how hot a car can get in the summer with the windows rolled up. If sunlight comes in and the heat cannot get out, the car can get dangerously hot.

Greenhouse gases do the same thing. They let the sunlight into Earth's atmosphere, but once the sunlight hits the ground and becomes heat, the gases then keep the heat in. This, called the greenhouse effect, makes Earth warmer.

Where do these greenhouse gases come from? One of the most common sources is **carbon dioxide**. This is what you and every other animal breathe out. Plants breathe in carbon dioxide, so it is important to the environment. However, cars and other machines make carbon dioxide as well, because they burn **fossil fuels** such as oil and coal. This means there is much more of this greenhouse gas being made today than 50 or 100 years ago.

Cars and the carbon dioxide they release are a big reason for the increase in greenhouse gases.

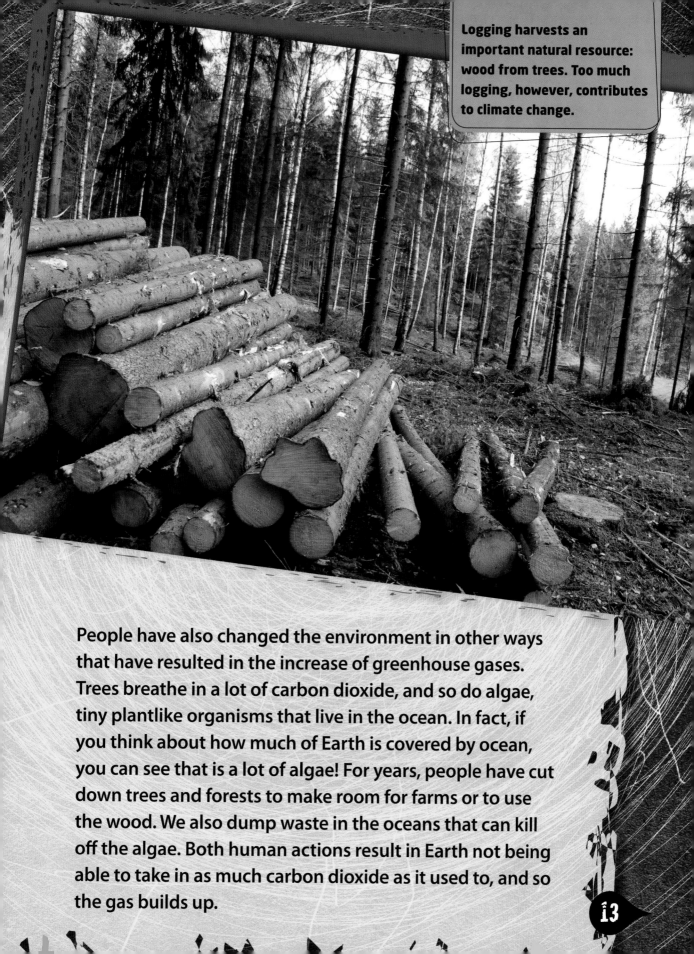

People have also changed the environment in other ways that have resulted in the increase of greenhouse gases. Trees breathe in a lot of carbon dioxide, and so do algae, tiny plantlike organisms that live in the ocean. In fact, if you think about how much of Earth is covered by ocean, you can see that is a lot of algae! For years, people have cut down trees and forests to make room for farms or to use the wood. We also dump waste in the oceans that can kill off the algae. Both human actions result in Earth not being able to take in as much carbon dioxide as it used to, and so the gas builds up.

Effects of Climate Change

We have seen some of the problems that polar bears are facing. How can the climate cause these problems?

Even a small change in a climate's temperature can cause big changes later. The change between water freezing and melting is only one degree. So climate change begins with how Earth stays warm or cool: the oceans.

Oceans cover almost three-fourths of Earth's surface. More than half of all living things are found in our oceans. Oceans are also important to animals that live primarily on land. For example, polar bears hunt seals, and many types of birds eat fish that live in the ocean.

Coral reefs, like this one, are vulnerable to rising water temperatures.

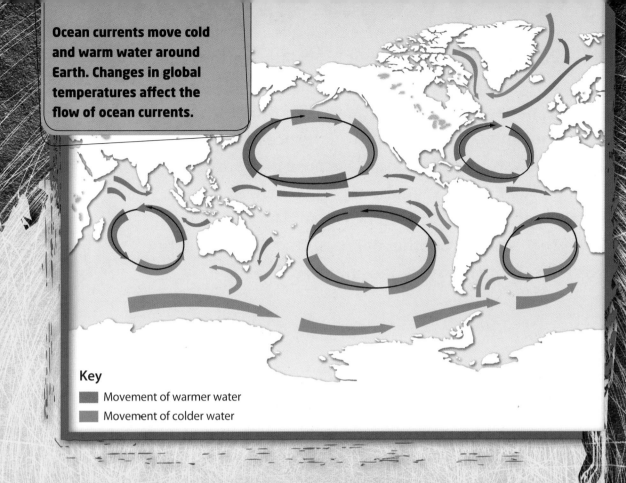

Ocean currents move cold and warm water around Earth. Changes in global temperatures affect the flow of ocean currents.

Key
- Movement of warmer water
- Movement of colder water

Ocean currents are caused by different water temperatures, which are made by the heat of the sun. Cold water is heavier than warm water, so it sinks to the bottom of the ocean. As cold water sinks, warmer water moves into its place.

The **Gulf Stream** is an important ocean current between North America and Europe. It moves warm water from the eastern coast of North America to the western coast of Europe.

The Gulf Stream water heats the air above it. When the warm air moves inland, it brings mild temperatures and rain throughout the year.

The warm water of the Gulf Stream attracts many kinds of fish and activity wherever the current travels. Animals that are attracted to the food the Gulf Stream current brings are themselves food for larger animals.

When water that was cold becomes just a little warmer, the currents can change. When the climate becomes colder, the different varieties of fish will not go as far north or south as they used to. Animals that depend on the ocean currents for food and warmth will struggle. Because they are used to warmer water, these animals may find it hard to survive, especially since it can also become too cold for their food, whether that is plants or other animals. Changes in climate always affect more than just one animal.

As ocean currents warm, fish like this Atlantic cod move to new habitats in search of food and mates.

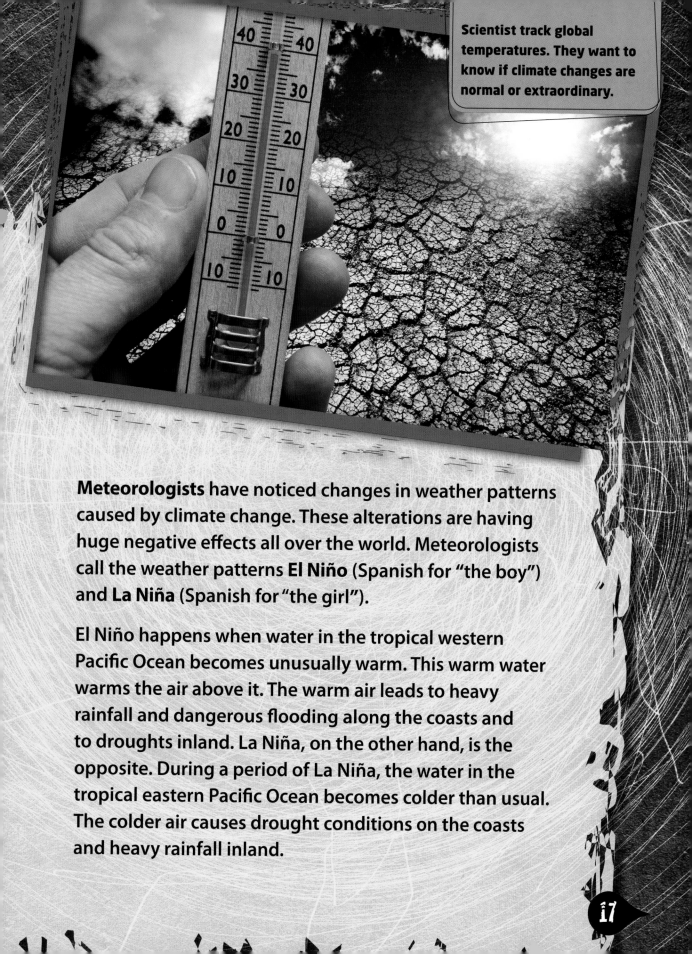

Meteorologists have noticed changes in weather patterns caused by climate change. These alterations are having huge negative effects all over the world. Meteorologists call the weather patterns **El Niño** (Spanish for "the boy") and **La Niña** (Spanish for "the girl").

El Niño happens when water in the tropical western Pacific Ocean becomes unusually warm. This warm water warms the air above it. The warm air leads to heavy rainfall and dangerous flooding along the coasts and to droughts inland. La Niña, on the other hand, is the opposite. During a period of La Niña, the water in the tropical eastern Pacific Ocean becomes colder than usual. The colder air causes drought conditions on the coasts and heavy rainfall inland.

Changing water temperatures in the ocean affect some fish and other sea creatures. Some animals do not like it when water temperatures change too much. Others cannot survive when water temperatures change. So they decide to move to find water that is closer to what they are used to.

As you have learned, all creatures live in particular habitats. They know how to live and thrive in those natural habitats. They know where to find food and mates. When animals are forced to move, they must change their ways of living. They have to find new places to live where they can survive. They have to find new sources of food and new mates.

Even the mighty shark is affected by climate change. Changing ocean currents affect where sharks breed and hunt.

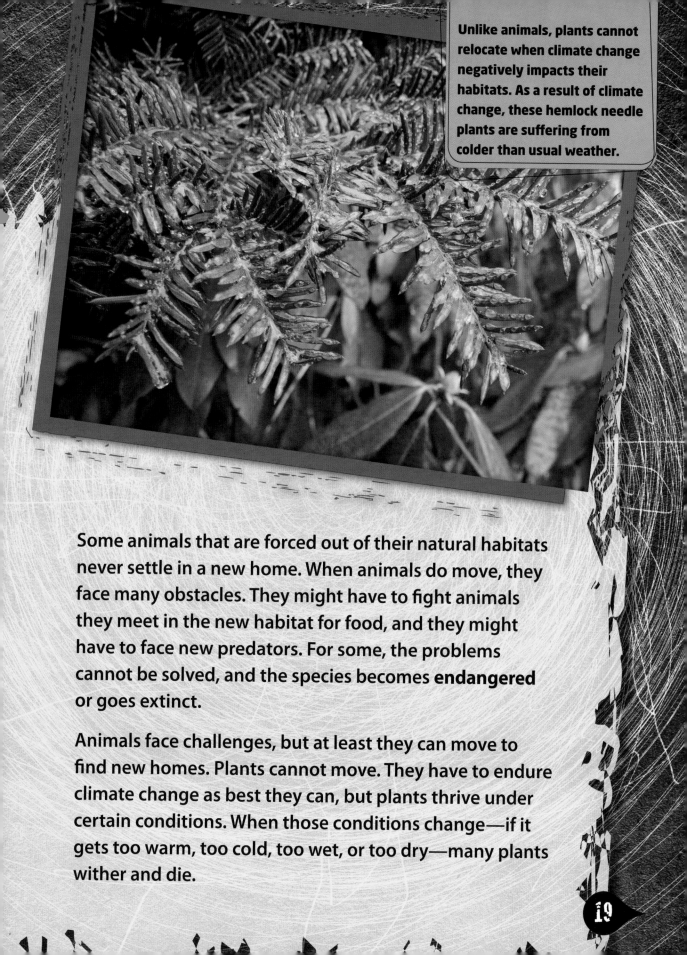

Unlike animals, plants cannot relocate when climate change negatively impacts their habitats. As a result of climate change, these hemlock needle plants are suffering from colder than usual weather.

Some animals that are forced out of their natural habitats never settle in a new home. When animals do move, they face many obstacles. They might have to fight animals they meet in the new habitat for food, and they might have to face new predators. For some, the problems cannot be solved, and the species becomes **endangered** or goes extinct.

Animals face challenges, but at least they can move to find new homes. Plants cannot move. They have to endure climate change as best they can, but plants thrive under certain conditions. When those conditions change—if it gets too warm, too cold, too wet, or too dry—many plants wither and die.

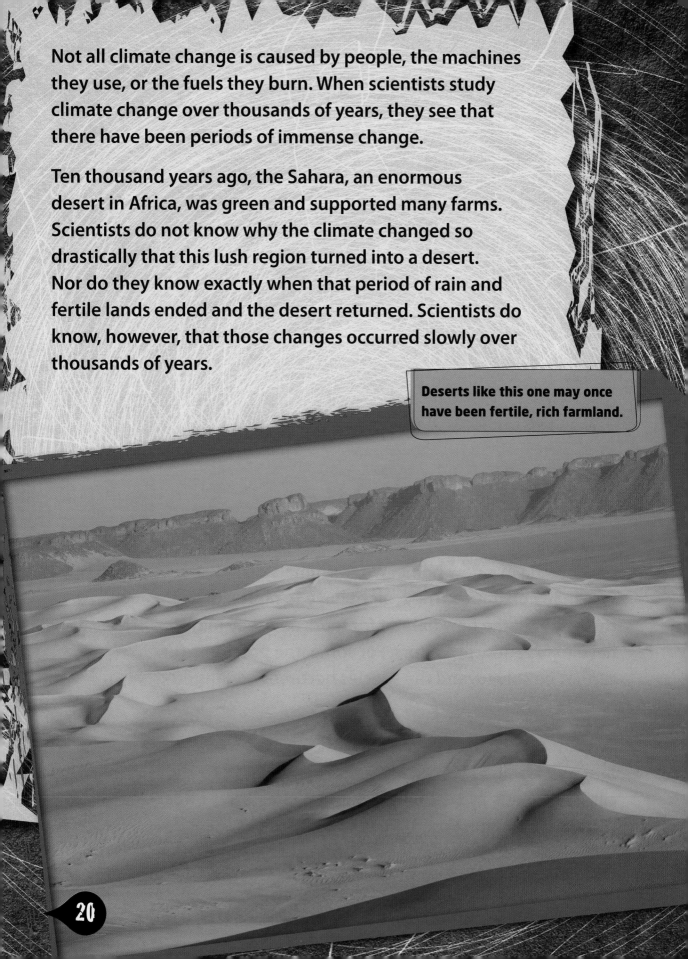

Not all climate change is caused by people, the machines they use, or the fuels they burn. When scientists study climate change over thousands of years, they see that there have been periods of immense change.

Ten thousand years ago, the Sahara, an enormous desert in Africa, was green and supported many farms. Scientists do not know why the climate changed so drastically that this lush region turned into a desert. Nor do they know exactly when that period of rain and fertile lands ended and the desert returned. Scientists do know, however, that those changes occurred slowly over thousands of years.

Deserts like this one may once have been fertile, rich farmland.

Residents clean up after a massive storm.

Some meteorologists wonder if climate change is making storms more ferocious, turning them into super storms. They point to Hurricane Sandy as an example. Hurricanes in the Atlantic are not rare, but Sandy was a monster. The largest Atlantic hurricane on record, Sandy hit the northeastern United States in late October 2012. This single storm caused over $70 billion in damage.

Scientists will not say that climate change caused Hurricane Sandy. But some will say that climate change made the storm bigger than it would have been normally.

Changes in the climate are also having an effect on water levels in the oceans around the world. Scientists may not agree on the reasons, but they do agree that sea levels around the world are rising. One reason for the rise is that as objects get warmer, they expand. This is true of the water in the oceans. As ocean waters warm, they expand in volume.

Another reason for the rise in ocean levels is the melting of giant glaciers. Glaciers melt slowly, but scientists warn that if global warming continues to increase, the rate at which glaciers melt will also increase. The rise in the sea level could perhaps one day be measured in feet and not inches.

This map shows that the polar ice cap is shrinking.

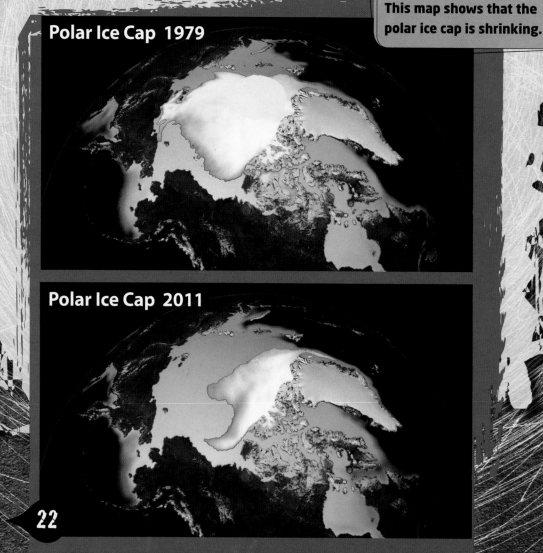

Polar Ice Cap 1979

Polar Ice Cap 2011

Prolonged drought in the Midwest has caused the Mississippi River to shrink.

In 2012, the same year Hurricane Sandy pummeled the states along the East Coast with rain and floods, the middle of the United States was suffering the effects of long-term drought. This drought was the worst in 50 years. In some areas, the drought was well into its second year.

One effect of the drought in the Midwest is that the giant Mississippi River is running low. Its water level is so low that barge and ship traffic may have to be suspended.

Many people are used to seeing flocks of birds flying south for the winter. They are migrating—moving from one region to another. Climate change is affecting how animals migrate. How do animals know when it is time to move from one region to another region? They rely on the weather. When the weather gets cold, many species of birds fly to warmer areas. Other land animals move to lower elevations.

Climate change is making a difference in the times that animals migrate. Summers are lasting longer and winters are getting less severe. Animals will not know when to migrate if climate change continues to affect weather patterns.

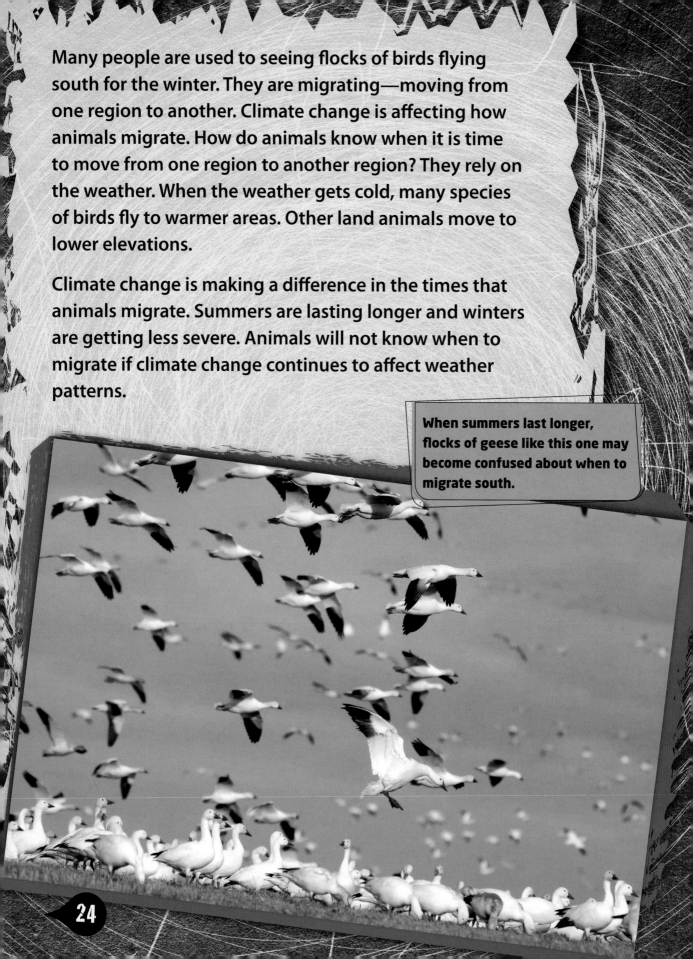

When summers last longer, flocks of geese like this one may become confused about when to migrate south.

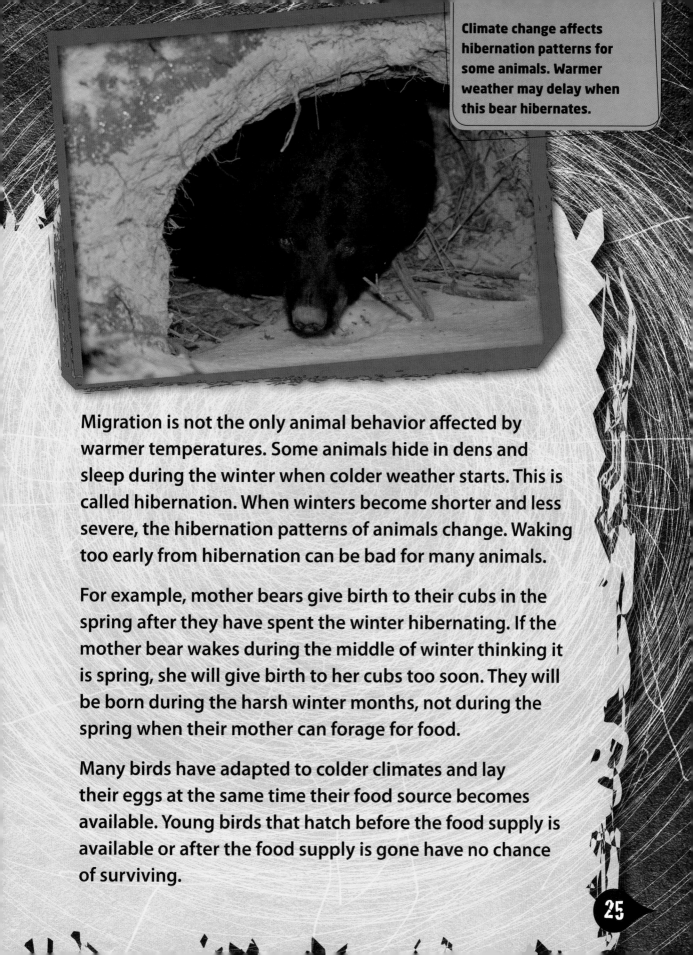

Climate change affects hibernation patterns for some animals. Warmer weather may delay when this bear hibernates.

Migration is not the only animal behavior affected by warmer temperatures. Some animals hide in dens and sleep during the winter when colder weather starts. This is called hibernation. When winters become shorter and less severe, the hibernation patterns of animals change. Waking too early from hibernation can be bad for many animals.

For example, mother bears give birth to their cubs in the spring after they have spent the winter hibernating. If the mother bear wakes during the middle of winter thinking it is spring, she will give birth to her cubs too soon. They will be born during the harsh winter months, not during the spring when their mother can forage for food.

Many birds have adapted to colder climates and lay their eggs at the same time their food source becomes available. Young birds that hatch before the food supply is available or after the food supply is gone have no chance of surviving.

Some animals' appearance also changes each season. For example, the fur color of snowshoe rabbits changes twice a year. The rabbits are brown in the summer and white in the winter. This helps hide them all year long from predators that hunt them for food.

The fur of snowshoe rabbits changes color according to the temperature, which is based on how much sunlight there is. The problem comes when the fur color of these rabbits changes, but the weather is too warm for snow. The now-white rabbits are easily seen by wolves and other predators.

Climate change may alter the time of year when this snowshoe rabbit changes the color of its fur.

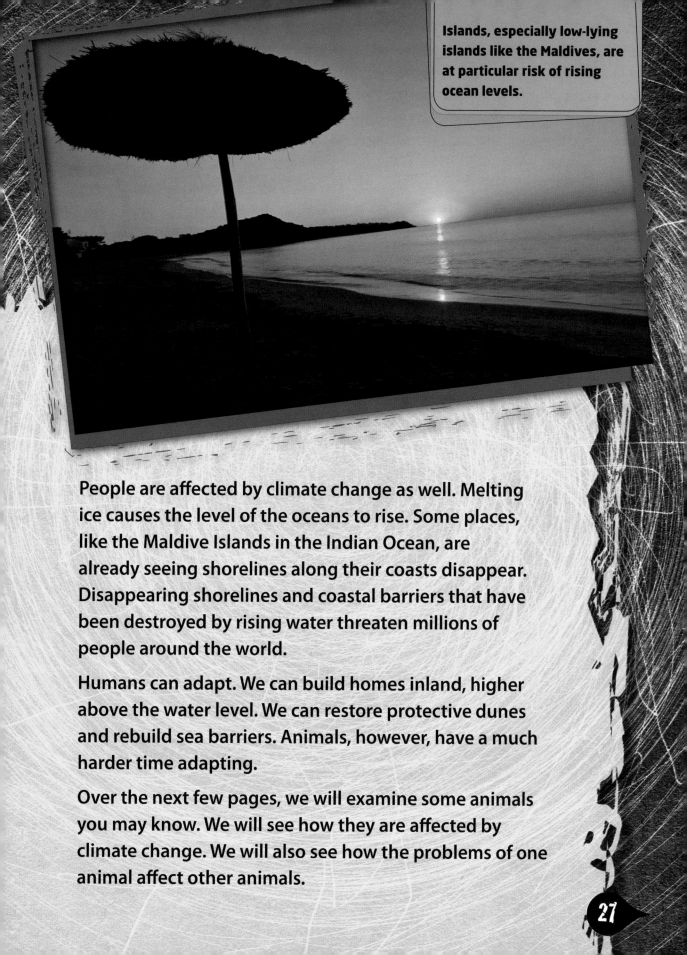

People are affected by climate change as well. Melting ice causes the level of the oceans to rise. Some places, like the Maldive Islands in the Indian Ocean, are already seeing shorelines along their coasts disappear. Disappearing shorelines and coastal barriers that have been destroyed by rising water threaten millions of people around the world.

Humans can adapt. We can build homes inland, higher above the water level. We can restore protective dunes and rebuild sea barriers. Animals, however, have a much harder time adapting.

Over the next few pages, we will examine some animals you may know. We will see how they are affected by climate change. We will also see how the problems of one animal affect other animals.

Polar Bears

Polar bears have adapted well to the harsh conditions of the Arctic. Because their white fur helps them blend in with the ice and the snow, they are able to sneak up on seals and other prey. They use floating ice sheets as hunting platforms and resting areas.

Polar bears, however, are in serious trouble. Polar ice is crucial to their way of life. Warmer temperatures, one of the results of climate change, are causing the polar ice to melt. Today there are fewer ice sheets than just a few years ago, and many of them are too thin for polar bears to stand on. Without ice sheets to provide a place to rest during their hunts for seals and fish, polar bears have to swim farther and farther.

Polar bears are great swimmers, but they cannot swim for long lengths of time. With no place to climb out of the water and rest, they end up drowning. Polar ice is critical to the survival of polar bears.

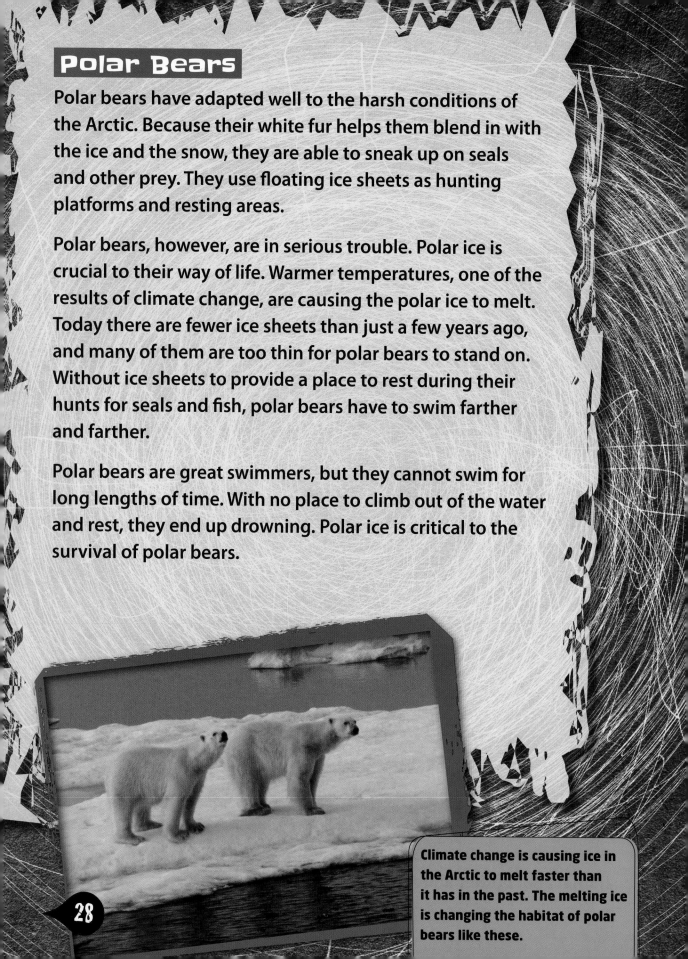

Climate change is causing ice in the Arctic to melt faster than it has in the past. The melting ice is changing the habitat of polar bears like these.

Melting Arctic ice means that polar bears have to swim much farther than they are used to when hunting for food.

Scientists point to the polar bear as an example of the impact climate change is having on our planet.

When polar bears cannot catch enough food, they become weak and sick. Like all other animals, they will starve without food. When mother polar bears die or are too weak to hunt, they are not able to feed their cubs. As a result, the next generation of polar bears becomes smaller, and the next generation even smaller. These problems have caused polar bears to become endangered. The number of polar bears is so small that scientists are worried they might all die out.

Penguins

At the bottom of Earth, as far south from the polar bears as one can get, you can find penguins in Antarctica. Like so many other animals, these flightless birds are well suited to their environment. For penguins, however, it is a cold, icy world.

Penguins look strange when they walk, but they are amazing when they are in the water. Their wings allow them to swim fast and deep. Because they can nearly fly through the water, they are superb hunters of fish.

In the warmer, northern area of Antarctic, along the Antarctic Peninsula, Adélie penguins depend on the sea ice. But their habitat is disappearing because of climate change.

A mother penguin feeds her chick.

Emperor penguins live at the South Pole. Like polar bears that live at the North Pole, emperor penguins also depend on ice. These penguins breed and give birth to their chicks on ice sheets. The ice protects the baby emperor penguins from the cold waters beneath and around the ice.

As a result of the warmer temperatures, ice sheets at the South Pole are beginning to break apart sooner than the penguins are used to. This is creating a problem for the penguins and their chicks. Because the ice is breaking up early, chicks do not have the time they need to grow up on the ice. They are not yet ready to swim in the icy waters. As the ice sheets break apart, many of the chicks are swept away and drown.

Adélie penguins also live at the South Pole. The problem they face is not that ice breaks up too soon. Their problem is too much snow!

Adélie penguins do not lay their eggs on ice like emperor penguins. Instead, they lay their eggs on barren, rocky ground that does not have any snow. One strange effect of climate change is that warmer air is causing more snow to fall at the South Pole. Too much snow means that Adélie penguins cannot find snow-free rocky ground on which to lay their eggs. Many of their eggs freeze when they come in contact with the snow. The babies are lost even before they hatch.

Climate change is making life for penguins more difficult. They have to work harder to find food.

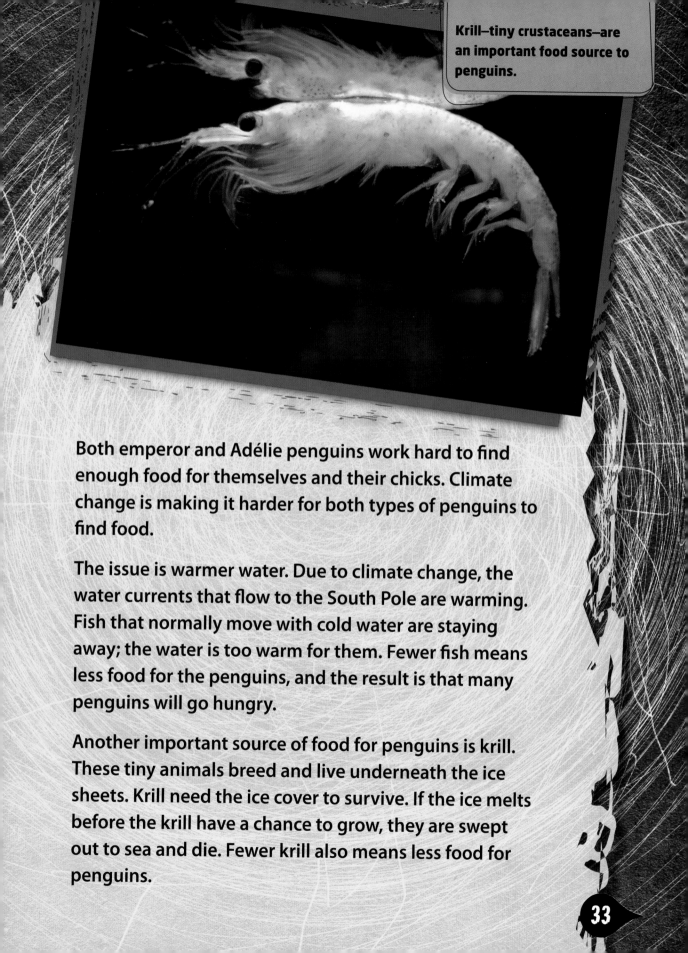

Krill—tiny crustaceans—are an important food source to penguins.

Both emperor and Adélie penguins work hard to find enough food for themselves and their chicks. Climate change is making it harder for both types of penguins to find food.

The issue is warmer water. Due to climate change, the water currents that flow to the South Pole are warming. Fish that normally move with cold water are staying away; the water is too warm for them. Fewer fish means less food for the penguins, and the result is that many penguins will go hungry.

Another important source of food for penguins is krill. These tiny animals breed and live underneath the ice sheets. Krill need the ice cover to survive. If the ice melts before the krill have a chance to grow, they are swept out to sea and die. Fewer krill also means less food for penguins.

Clown Fish

You may have seen clown fish in an aquarium. They are easy to spot because of their bright colors. Clown fish are in danger from climate change, too. Clown fish live in a very specific habitat—coral reefs. The hard skeletons of millions of coral animals create coral reefs, and the reefs exist only where the water is warm. The water cannot be too warm, however—a one-degree increase in temperature can kill coral reefs.

Earlier we discussed the impact of carbon dioxide on climate change. When carbon dioxide moves from air into water, it makes coral unhealthy. Unhealthy coral affect the thousands of different types of sea creatures, including clown fish, that can live only in that habitat.

Coral reefs are home to many sea creatures, such as these clown fish. Coral reefs are in danger from waters warmed by climate change.

A turtle lays her eggs on a beach. Disappearing shorelines and sandy beaches are threatening turtle populations.

Sea Turtles

Many animals need a very special kind of habitat for their young. Sea turtles, for instance, need a special kind of beach on which to lay their eggs. But, as the ice at the North and the South Poles melts, the ocean levels rise. The higher water decreases the size of the sandy beaches where turtles lay their eggs. It can even wash away the beaches completely.

The problem of disappearing beaches is compounded by the fact that while sea turtles migrate during the year, females return to the beaches where they were born to lay their eggs. They use ocean currents to help direct them back to those locations. But as you have read, ocean currents are changing. Now, turtles might struggle to locate the same beach where they were born and where they laid their eggs in the past.

Sharks

Sharks have lived in the oceans for millions of years, since the time of the dinosaurs! While sharks have been on Earth for a long time, they face a new problem: people.

People and sharks both enjoy warm water, but if the water becomes too warm, sharks can become ill.

People on this beach attempt to lure these pup sharks closer. Human-shark contact is almost always bad for both groups.

As oceans become warmer, sharks swim to water where they feel more at home. But this brings them close to where people fish, swim, and surf.

Human-shark contact is always bad for one species or the other. Sharks have been known to attack swimmers and surfers. People are so afraid of sharks that they want them killed on sight.

Pandas

Pandas are one of the most endangered animals today. Their food is threatened and so is their territory.

Pandas live in a very small region in China, where they eat a diet of bamboo. Changes in rainfall mean that the bamboo forests there are suffering. There is not enough bamboo to support the panda population.

People have tried to help fix this problem by planting new bamboo forests in other places. But China is growing rapidly, and towns and cities are spreading. It is becoming harder to find new, natural locations where pandas can survive and thrive.

Although Pandas prefer bamboo, they will eat other plants.

Blue Whales

The blue whale is the largest animal on Earth, but its food is one of the smallest animals in the ocean: krill. Blue whales can eat more than 40 million krill in a day. That is almost 8,000 pounds (3,628 kg). Even these giant creatures face problems from climate change.

Melting polar ice affects ocean currents which impacts the number of krill, the primary food source of blue whales. Blue whales also migrate. While they are in cold waters, they eat as much krill as they can find. However, they give birth and raise their young (called calves) in warmer waters. The rising ocean temperatures can change their migration paths.

Bees

They might not look like it, but bees are among the most important insects when it comes to the food you eat. Bees pollinate plants and flowers, so apples, tomatoes, roses, and raspberries are all helped by the bees flying from blossom to blossom.

These helpers come out every spring to work, but climate change has caused problems for bees. Some types of bees, like many other insects, sleep during the winter and wake up in the spring when the blossoms on the trees and plants come out.

A honeybee sips nectar from a flower.

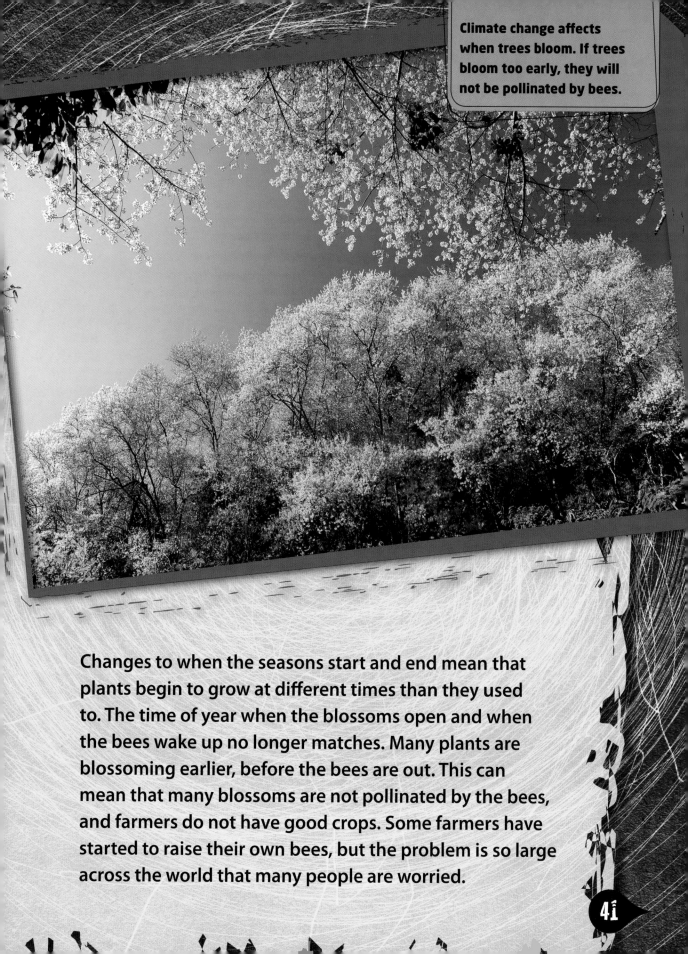

Climate change affects when trees bloom. If trees bloom too early, they will not be pollinated by bees.

Changes to when the seasons start and end mean that plants begin to grow at different times than they used to. The time of year when the blossoms open and when the bees wake up no longer matches. Many plants are blossoming earlier, before the bees are out. This can mean that many blossoms are not pollinated by the bees, and farmers do not have good crops. Some farmers have started to raise their own bees, but the problem is so large across the world that many people are worried.

41

What Can We Do?

It is hard to read about the animals that inhabit our planet and not feel we must do something about their future. But what can we do? It may seem impossible to help, but just knowing how our actions can affect Earth's climate is a good step. A big part of this is knowing that we are all part of nature. We need all kinds of animals, even those we might not otherwise think of, like krill or coral.

A healthy climate means a healthy planet.

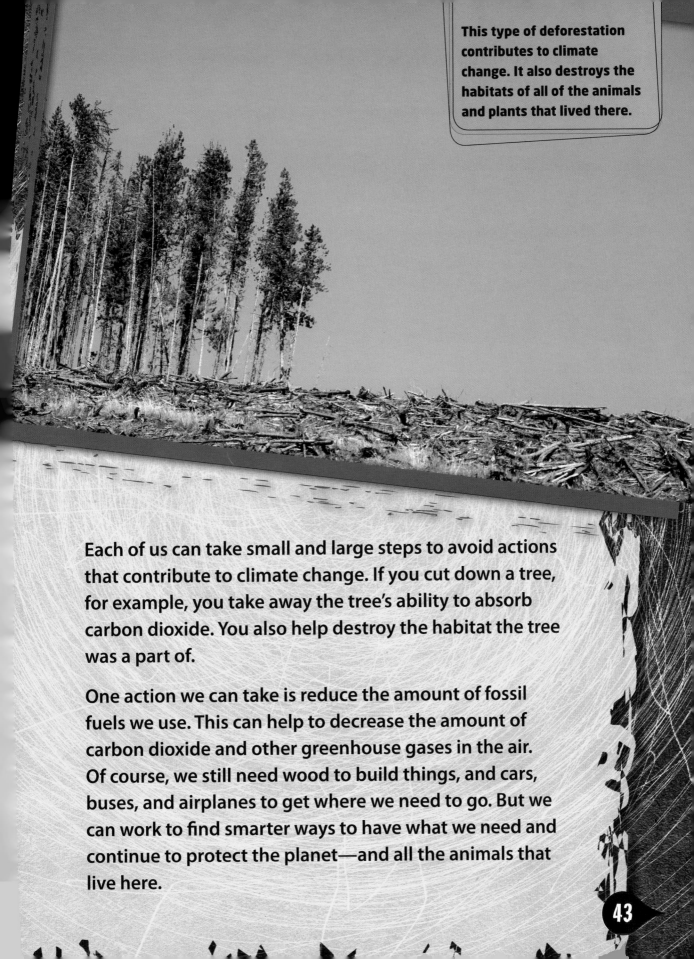

This type of deforestation contributes to climate change. It also destroys the habitats of all of the animals and plants that lived there.

Each of us can take small and large steps to avoid actions that contribute to climate change. If you cut down a tree, for example, you take away the tree's ability to absorb carbon dioxide. You also help destroy the habitat the tree was a part of.

One action we can take is reduce the amount of fossil fuels we use. This can help to decrease the amount of carbon dioxide and other greenhouse gases in the air. Of course, we still need wood to build things, and cars, buses, and airplanes to get where we need to go. But we can work to find smarter ways to have what we need and continue to protect the planet—and all the animals that live here.

Finally, we can come up with new and different solutions to fight climate change. When we replant trees wiped out by deforestation, we take carbon dioxide out of the atmosphere. Less carbon dioxide means lower temperatures. New trees also provide new homes and habitats for insects and wildlife.

Although we can find new homes for animals affected by climate change, the best way to help them is to protect the habitats they already have.

A worker plants tree seedlings. Planting trees is a positive way to respond to deforestation.

We can find ways to live in harmony with our planet. It is the only one we have!

Climate change happens in our own backyard, but it also happens in faraway places. All parts of Earth are connected to each other. Melting ice sheets in the Arctic affect the Gulf Stream off the coast of Florida, which in turn affects the climate in Ireland. The largest animals need the smallest, and busy bees provide food for everyone.

As you can see, doing our part to understand and to slow climate change will end up helping everyone and everything.

Glossary

atmosphere: the mass of air that surrounds Earth

carbon dioxide: colorless, odorless gas formed during respiration

climate: average weather conditions, measured over a long period of time

climate change: long-term change in Earth's climate

El Niño: abnormally warm water in the tropical western Pacific Ocean that causes unusually heavy rainfall on the Pacific coasts and dry conditions inland

endangered: species in danger of dying out within 20 years

environment: everything that affects an organism during its lifetime

extinct: no longer existing

fossil fuels: fuels such as coal, natural gas, or oil that were made from plants and animals that died millions of years ago

greenhouse gases: gases that trap heat in the atmosphere

Gulf Stream: a warm ocean current of the northern Atlantic Ocean off eastern North America

La Niña: abnormally cool water in the tropical western Pacific Ocean that causes unusually light rainfall on the Pacific coasts and wet conditions inland

meteorologists: scientists who study the weather

For More Information

Books

Cherry, Lynne. *How We Know What We Know About Our Changing Climate: Scientists and Kids Explore Global Warming*. Nevada City, CA: Dawn Publications, 2010.

French, Lisa. *Who Turned Up the Heat? Eco-Pig Explains Global Warming*. Minneapolis, MN: Magic Wagon Publishing, 2009.

Websites

Center for Climate and Energy Solutions
www.c2es.org/
Use this site to learn about research dedicated to safe, reliable, affordable energy for all while protecting the global climate.

Union of Concerned Scientists
www.ucsusa.org/
The goal of the Union of Concerned Scientists website is to help build a global movement to fight climate change.

Index